BRITAIN IN OLD P

BOULTON PAUL AIRCRAFT

A L E C   B R E W

ALAN SUTTON PUBLISHING LIMITED

Alan Sutton Publishing Limited
Phoenix Mill · Far Thrupp · Stroud
Gloucestershire · GL5 2BU

First Published 1995

Cover photograph: (front) The Boulton and
Paul P.6 at Mousehold in 1918; in the centre is
J.D. North, the Company's guiding light for
over fifty years; (back) a production Defiant,
NI673, on a test flight in 1939.

British Library Cataloguing in Publication Data.
A catalogue record for this book is available from
the British Library.

ISBN 0-7509-1028-3

Typeset in 9/10 Sabon.
Typesetting and origination by
Alan Sutton Publishing Limited.
Printed in Great Britain by
Ebenezer Baylis, Worcester.

Boulton & Paul's first design, the P.3 Bobolink fighter, at Mousehold airfield, 1918.
Around the flight sheds in the background are FE.2bs and Sopwith Camels, all built by
the company.

Contents

Boulton Paul's most famous product, the Defiant fighter, this one being N1550, the Mk II prototype, photographed in June 1940.

The Boulton Paul Defiant prototype, K8310, outside the flight sheds at Pendeford, Wolverhampton, just after its gun turret was fitted for the first time in January 1938.

Introduction

In 1995 Boulton Paul Aircraft celebrates eighty years in the aircraft industry, eighty years when many aircraft manufacturers with more illustrious names have disappeared. Surviving as a relatively small company by innovation and invention, Boulton Paul Aircraft has undergone two remarkable transformations in its existence.

It began life in 1915 as the aircraft department of Boulton & Paul Ltd, a long-established Norwich company. This had been formed as an ironmonger's in Cockey Lane, Norwich in 1797. It was not until 1844 that the name Boulton became associated with the firm, when William Staples Boulton became a partner, and not until 1853 that Joseph John Dawson Paul was taken on, firstly as an apprentice, much later as a partner. The company became renowned woodworkers, ironfounders, wire-netting manufacturers and steel erectors.

In 1915 the War Office brought them into aircraft manufacture with an initial order for 50 FE.2bs, a Royal Aircraft Factory design. The company built 550 in all, followed by more Sopwith Camels than anyone else, but, in 1917, decided to set up their own aircraft design department, and, to head it, engaged John Dudley North. He was one of the true pioneers of British aviation, having been made Chief Engineer at the Grahame White Company in 1913 at the tender age of twenty.

The Boulton & Paul aircraft department soon established a reputation for pioneering work in metal aircraft structure and as a manufacturer of high-performance twin-engined medium bombers, epitomized by the Sidestrand. They built the first aircraft with an all-metal structure ever delivered to the Royal Air Force, the P.15 Bolton, and the entire structure of the R.101 airship, the largest 'aircraft' ever built in this country.

During 1934–36 the first major transformation of the company took place. The aircraft department was sold off and became an independent company, Boulton Paul Aircraft Ltd, (without the '&'). Two years later it moved to a brand new factory at Pendeford, Wolverhampton, where it became a specialist in the manufacture of two-seat fighters and a range of electro-hydraulic gun turrets. Here was produced its most famous product, the Defiant fighter, which fought in the Battle of Britain alongside the Spitfire and Hurricane, and later as a successful night fighter.

Back in Norwich its former parent, Boulton & Paul Ltd, was brought back into aircraft manufacture during the Second World War as part of a consortium building the Airspeed Oxford and Horsa glider. After the war it returned to being one of the country's pre-eminent woodworking concerns, specializing today in the manufacture of doors and windows, and high quality fitted kitchens.

After the war Boulton Paul Aircraft attempted to transform itself again into a manufacturer of military trainer aircraft, with mixed success. Its future actually lay in the manufacture of power controls and other hydraulic systems, stemming directly from its gun-turret work. Its second transformation, into a manufacturer of high technology aeronautical equipment, was sealed with the merger in 1960 with the Dowty Group. The company emerged as Dowty Boulton Paul Ltd, now trading as Dowty Aerospace Wolverhampton.

Boulton Paul had flown the first aircraft in the world with electrical signalling on all three axes, the Tay-Viscount of 1958. It was to fly the ACT Jaguar, the first aircraft with an all-digital quadruplex flight-control system, with no mechanical back-up. Today, along with a sister company in California, it is one of the world's leaders in fly-by-wire control systems.

From braced-by-wire to fly-by-wire Boulton (&) Paul Aircraft has been at the forefront of aeronautical innovation for eighty years. It has generated a degree of pride in a workforce drawn from two quite different towns, Norwich and Wolverhampton. This pride is epitomized by the creation, in 1991, of a voluntary group, the Boulton Paul Association, dedicated to the preservation of the company's history.

I have to thank Putnam books for permission to include the eight photographs which also appeared in my book *Boulton Paul Aircraft since 1915*, which was a comprehensive history of the Company. As over two hundred of the photographs in this book have never been seen in print before, this book can be considered complementary to my Putnam book, but also stands in its own right as a pictorial history of a famous old company.

NORWICH

The Norwich company of Boulton & Paul Ltd was formed in 1797 and became
ironworkers, steelworkers and woodworkers specializing in pre-fabricated buildings. In
1915 they were invited to build aircraft and received their first order for fifty FE.2bs, a
two-seater designed at the Royal Aircraft Factory. They went on to build 550 in all. The
first one, illustrated here, serial 5201, was completed on 2 October 1915, but, because of
engine trouble, did not fly for the first time until 4 October. It was named 'Bombay 1',
having been paid for by the residents of that city.

The company's main Riverside Works in Norwich during the First World War. Aircraft were built here and then transported to the new airfield at Mousehold for erection and flight testing.

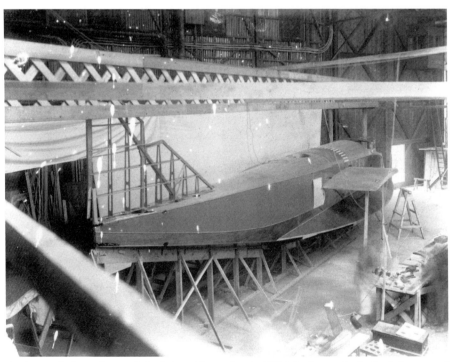

An internal view of part of the Riverside works in 1918. It shows the hull of the second Felixstowe F.3 flying boat built by Boulton & Paul. They built seventy Felixstowe hulls altogether, both F.3s and the slightly different F.5s.

Boulton & Paul, Limited,

Aeronautical Department, Norwich.

The Directors have pleasure in inviting

to inspect the first Aeroplane manufactured at Rose Lane Works, on the Military Aerodrome, Mousehold, Saturday Afternoon next, October 2nd, 1915.

It is hoped that a trial flight will be possible.

Kindly bring this Card with you to ensure admission to the Military Aerodrome.

TEA, COFFEE, AND . . LIGHT REFRESHMENTS.

An unused invitation for the unveiling of the first FE.2b built, 1915. 'Light refreshments' included champagne to celebrate the first flight, piloted by the famous Howard Pixton. The champagne was broached although the engine refused to start even after the mechanics had been trying for two embarrassing hours: the aircraft did not in fact fly until two days later.

Sopwith Camel FE6314 at RAF Abingdon, 1969. FE.2b/d was followed, on the Boulton & Paul production lines, by the Sopwith Camel, including this one. It is the sole surviving aircraft built by the company in Norwich and is now in the RAF Museum, Hendon.

Section of a photograph showing one week's production of Sopwith Camels in 1918, forty-three in all. This was not even the best week's production, which was a total of seventy in the week ending 20 July 1918. Boulton & Paul built 1,575 Camels, more than any other company, except Ruston-Proctor, which also built 1,575.

World record lift of ten people in a Grahame White Type 10 Charabanc, 2 October 1913. Boulton & Paul set up their own design department in 1917, and, to head it, recruited John Dudley North. He is seen here fourth from the left in the Grahame White Type 10 Charabanc, which he had designed. It was piloted on this occasion by Louis Noel, who is on the left.

This shield was presented to J.D. North on leaving Grahame White in 1915. He had become Chief Engineer in charge of seventy people there at the age of twenty. Later he became production superintendent at Austin Motors, laying down production lines for the RE.7.

The Bobolink when first erected at Riverside, December 1917. It was named after a North American bird and designed as the Sopwith Camel replacement with a Bentley BR.2 engine. It is shown without its cowling.

A rear view of the Bobolink also at Riverside, December 1917. This shows that the plane was originally fitted with a Lewis gun on a sliding rail, as well as the two fixed Vickers guns. The two fuel tanks, sited behind the cockpit, are not yet fitted.

The Bobolink at Mousehold for flight testing, 1918. Three were ordered but only C8655 completed. The Lewis gun has now been removed. In the background is a row of Camels, which were being built at an average of twenty-eight per week at the time.

The Bobolink at Martlesham Heath in March 1918 for trials against other potential 'Camel replacements'. Ailerons have now been added to the lower wings. The Bobolink lost out to the rival Sopwith Snipe in winning orders.

ERECTING SHEDS

– AND –

HANGARS

A page from a company brochure showing Sopwith Snipes being erected at Mousehold, *c.* 1918. Boulton & Paul received orders for 500 Snipes, but had only completed 425 when orders were curtailed after the war.

The rather primitive way in which Snipes were transported from Riverside to Mousehold for erection.

One of the company's hangars at Mousehold, full of Snipes, *c*. 1918: an enlargement of the brochure on the previous page. Production of the Snipe went on well into 1919.

The sole Boulton & Paul P.6, serial number X-25, 1918. It was built to test aerofoil sections. Well wrapped up is director's wife Mrs Dawson Paul, ready to embark on her first flight.

Mrs Dawson Paul in the back seat of the P.6. It was being flown by the freelance test pilot Frank Courtney, who did most of the company's early testing.

Company transport, 1919. After the war the P.6 was put into use for the company. It had the honour of making the first official business flight in this country, on the day the Air Navigation Act came into effect, 1 May 1919. The sales manager flew to Bury St Edmunds and back, completing a deal.

A model of the P.7 Bourges (named after a French town), showing the twin Lewis guns in nose and dorsal positions.

A close-up of one of the BR.2 rotary engines fitted to the first Bourges, F2903, because the ABC Dragonfly radials for which it was designed were not ready. It was photographed in November 1918.

F2903 at Mousehold. The Dragonfly engines have now been fitted, together with huge spinners. The bomb-aiming position can be seen in the nose of the aircraft.

F2903 with the spinners removed because of the cooling problems suffered by the Dragonfly engine. Delays caused by the engines were enough to prevent the Bourges receiving production orders before the end of the war.

F2903 was the first of three Bourges prototypes ordered, all with slightly differing configurations. They were designated medium bombers and also fighter/bombers, such was their high performance.

Cecil Browne, the aircraft's engine mechanic, in the nose of the Bourges in flight, taken by the pilot. The Bourges was outstandingly aerobatic for a twin-engined aircraft, and Browne was noted for calmly occupying this position while the plane was looped and rolled.

The view of the Bourges port engine taken from the pilot's cockpit, just in front of the wings. The BR.2 engines indicate that this was taken in 1918.

Bourges F2903 being pulled up into a loop by Frank Courtney, probably with Cecil Browne in the front cockpit. Air-to-air photographs were very rare at this period.

Upside-down at the top of the loop high over the Norfolk countryside. The Bourges was the first fully aerobatic twin-engined aircraft.

A rear view of the first Bourges showing its straight upper wing, and the mid-gap position of the Dragonfly radials.

A rear view of the second prototype, F2904, 1919. This shows the gulled centre section which was designed to give the gunner a greater field of fire and the pilot a better rearward view. The tailplane gives a matching degree of dihedral. The Dragonfly engines were, in this case, mounted on the lower wing.

F2904 upside down after crashing at Mousehold early in 1919. The remains were salvaged and used in the construction of the second P.8 Atlantic.

The third and last Bourges, F2905, photographed late in 1919. This was powered by 450 hp Napier Lion engines mounted on the lower wing, but had the straight upper wing of the first prototype.

The P.8 Atlantic under construction early in 1919. After the war Boulton & Paul decided to mount a challenge for the £10,000 prize put up by Lord Northcliffe of the *Daily Mail* in 1913 for the first non-stop flight by heavier-than-air machines over the Atlantic. The aircraft was based on the Bourges, and used parts of the F2904.

The P.8 Atlantic was also to be the prototype for a new airliner seating eight passengers. This is a contemporary drawing of the airliner version taking off from Mousehold.

Close-up of one of the Napier Lion engines of the P.8 Atlantic. The plane was capable of flying on only one engine, unlike most other twin-engined aircraft of the day: a vital safety feature for the Atlantic flight.

Frank Courtney prepares the P.8 for its first flight in April 1919, with Cecil Browne in the cabin. Because some distinguished visitors wished to catch their train back to London, he omitted to run up both engines at the same time.

Because of a fuel supply problem one engine cut on take-off and the P.8 crashed. This ended any chance Boulton & Paul had of shipping it to Newfoundland to fly back in time to beat Alcock and Brown. The latter made the first Atlantic flight in a Vickers Vimy converted First World War bomber on 14/15 June 1919.

A close-up of the crashed P.8. A second aircraft was built as the prototype airliner, but no orders were forthcoming because it was overpowered for the seating capacity.

The second strand of the company's post-war strategy was an enlarged version of the P.6, shown under construction in 1919. The P.9 was powered by the same 90 hp RAF 1a engine. Like most manufacturers Boulton & Paul hoped that there would be a private flying boom.

A total of eight P.9s were built, four being exported to Australia, but it was impossible to compete with a new aircraft against dirt-cheap war-surplus machines. This one, G-EAPD, replaced the P.6 as the company aircraft for a while in 1919–20.

The P.9 was a well-thought-out design with useful performance. This view shows the two built-in suitcases sited just behind the rear cockpit.

The P.9, G-EAWS. This replaced G-EAPD as the company aircraft and flew in a number of air races. It survived until Easter 1929, when it crashed after the old RAF engine shed a cylinder in a race at Lympne.

An elaborate mock-up of an amphibian designed to an official specification in 1919. It was to be powered by a Napier Lion engine, and is shown here with the wheels down.

The mock-up at Riverside. The wheels are up, and the proximity of the pilot and gunner's cockpits can be clearly seen.

A Geoffrey Watson impression of a three-seater, all-steel, army co-operation aircraft designed in 1921. Following official policy at the time the fuel tanks are over the upper wings rather than in the fuselage.

J.D. North, Head of Aircraft Design, two colleagues with a theodolite, and a balloon, on the compass-swinging circle at Mousehold. What they are doing is anyone's guess, but throughout his career, North was interested in solving theoretical problems, and often employed a mathematician for just this purpose.

A page from a company brochure showing some of the extensive equipment installed at Riverside and the Rose Lane works (see p. 14).

The Paris Air Show, December 1919. After the war J.D. North decided that the future lay in metal construction and built the P.10, an all-steel, two-seater light aircraft, with Bakelite-Dilecto (i.e. plastic) fuselage panels. It was said to be the sensation of the Paris Air Show from a constructional viewpoint.

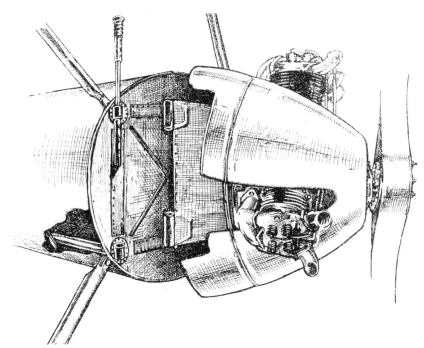

Contemporary sketch of the P.10's 100hp Cosmos Lucifer engine's swinging mount. This was a novel idea and allowed ease of maintenance at the rear of the engine.

Centre section of P.12 Bodmin J6910. In 1920 Boulton & Paul were awarded a contract to build two twin-engined aircraft to test the concept of siting the engines in a fuselage 'engine room' and driving wing-mounted propellers by a series of shafts and gears. These two photographs show the centre section, including the engine room, of the first of these P.12 Bodmins being taken from Riverside to Mousehold for erection in 1922.

The completed all-steel Bodmin, 1922. It was designated a 'Postal' aircraft for secrecy reasons, but it was really a prototype bomber..

Boulton & Paul were rewarded for their pioneering work in metal construction with an order for a version of the Bourges with an all-steel airframe, the P.15 Bolton. This is the fuselage frame of the aircraft in 1922.

The metal-framed P.15 Bolton, 1922. The aircraft has been erected without covering to show off its metal frame. It was to be the first all-metal aircraft ever delivered to the RAF.

A rear view of Bolton J6584, the sole prototype. Apart from its general layout it actually bore little resemblance to the Bourges.

J6984, the prototype Bugle, 1923. The Bolton was followed by an order for another all-metal three-seater medium bomber, the P.25 Bugle. This is J6984, the first prototype at Mousehold, where it flew for the first time on 25 July 1923. A P.12 Bodmin is in the hangar behind.

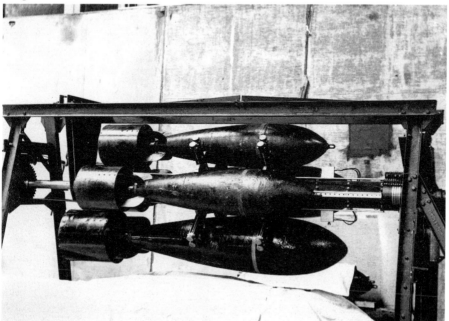

The Bugle's bomb rack. A novel revolving bomb rack was designed for the Bugle, which was also equipped with nose and dorsal gun positions.

One of the Jupiter engines of the Bugle, 1923. There were a total of five Jupiter-powered versions built.

The Bugle was fitted with this swinging engine mount as pioneered on the P.10 (see p. 33), for ease of maintenance. This allowed equipment at the rear of the engine to be reached without removing it from the airframe.

J7266 at Martlesham Heath for evaluation, *c.* 1928. The last two of a total of seven Bugles built were fitted with Napier Lion engines on the lower wings, in the manner of the Bolton, and designated P.25a Bugle IIs.

Boulton & Paul's 1st XI football team and sub-committee at the Newmarket Road sports pavilion, 1930. Back row first and second left are Joe Reed and Bill Monument, and the manager is wearing the flat cap. The front row is believed to be the sub-committee, not the forward line!

CAPT. J. D. PAUL
(Chairman)

HENRY FFISKE

W. H. FFISKE

J. J. D. PAUL D.L., J.P.

G. E. FFISKE

J. D. NORTH F.R. Ae.S.
M.I. Ae. E., F. R. Met. Soc.

STANLEY HOWES

The directors of Boulton & Paul, 1928. The Dawson Paul family had bought out the interests of William Staples Boulton in 1879. The ffiske family became partners in 1893 and Stanley Howes joined Boulton & Paul when the Aircraft Department was set up. J.D. North was shortly to become Managing Director.

In 1925 the company was awarded the contract to design and build the structure of the largest 'aircraft' ever built in this country, the R.101 airship. It was eventually to be 777 ft long. This is one of the triangular ridge girders.

Numerous R.101 girders at Boulton & Paul, c. 1925. They are awaiting transportation to the Royal Airship Works at Cardington, where they were erected. Boulton & Paul's part of the project went entirely to plan, unlike most other aspects.

The R.101 in the air over Norfolk. The cumulated problems which beset the project ended when R.101 crashed at Beauvais, France on 30 October 1930, on its maiden flight to India.

Another air-to-air view of the R.101, probably taken from the rear seat of Boulton & Paul's P.9.

Boulton & Paul's continued refinement of the high performance twin-engined medium bomber theme finally won them a production order for the P.29 Sidestrand.

A Sidestrand wing, outside the hangar at Mousehold. This was made by the Company's well refined locked-joint process. This process produced steel tubes by rolling a steel strip with one edge locked into a bead on the other.

The nose of the Sidestrand could be folded as here. This allowed access to the gunner/bomb-aimer's position.

The first of eighteen production Sidestrands, J9176, in 1928, which followed the two prototypes. There were nose, dorsal and ventral gun positions; the upper and lower decking was painted green to cut down glare from the otherwise silver doped fabric.

Front view of a Sidestrand Mk II. It shows the slim lines of the fuselage which helped to give the aircraft its high performance.

Similar view of a Sidestrand Mk III. This shows the revised bomb-aimer's position in the nose, and the more powerful Bristol Jupiter engines. It also has four-blade propellers.

Later Sidestrands were fitted with Townend rings, which cut down the drag of the engines considerably. Boulton & Paul were the company chosen to exploit Dr H.C.H. Townend's invention.

A production Sidestrand II, J9181. Like Boulton & Paul's previous medium bombers the Sidestrand was fully aerobatic, and could loop, roll and spin.

Sidestrands equipped just one RAF squadron: no. 101. In this cartoon squadron members seem quite happy with their mount, with which they were equipped from 1928 to 1933.

No. 101 squadron on manoeuvres in France. Four Sidestrand Mk IIIs are visible in the picture.

This is actually the second prototype Sidestrand, J7939, but brought up to Mk III standards. The servo rudder behind the main rudder was added to ease the heaviness of the control.

The first prototype P.31 Bittern, J7936, in 1928. This was a single-seater twin-engined monoplane fighter, well ahead of its time in concept, but rather underpowered with 230 hp Lynx engines. Only two were built. The second had Lewis guns in revolving barbettes on each side of the nose instead of the fixed Vickers guns shown here.

The sole P.32 three-engined heavy bomber, J9950, which first flew on 23 October 1931. This was the biggest aircraft Boulton & Paul ever built, powered by three 575 hp Bristol Jupiter XFBM radials.

This special engine hoist was designed to attach to the P.32's wing to enable the inaccessible centre engine to be changed.

An artist's impression of the P.33 Partridge fighter in flight. This was based on a photograph of the aircraft on the ground. Designed by Boulton & Paul it was one of several competing to replace the RAF's Siskins and Gamecocks. The orders eventually went to the Bristol Bulldog.

J.D. North (right) as a Royal Aero Club official at Mousehold during the King's Cup Air Race, 1930. He is talking to Mutt Summers, the pilot of the competing Vickers 141 fighter. Norwich was one of the first stops in the race.

The Vickers 141 being refuelled. Mutt Summers' parachute is lying on the grass. Summers had been one of the Martlesham Heath pilots who evaluated the competing fighters, but had just become Vickers' test pilot.

The sole P.33 Partridge, J8459. This and the Bobolink were Boulton & Paul's only single-seater, single-engined fighters.

The company's second venture into the light aircraft market, the P.41 Phoenix, in 1929 or 1930. It was powered by a 40 hp ABC Scorpion engine and would be flying very near to Mousehold, as pilots did not trust the little engine very far afield.

Boulton & Paul's sports and social committee outside the Newmarket Road sports pavilion, 1930.

The completely rebuilt Phoenix in 1931. It had an all-metal fuselage, more substantial undercarriage and a 40 hp Salmson radial engine. The company's chief test pilot, Sqd-Ldr Rea, used it as his personal runabout after the loss of his P.9. No orders were forthcoming for the Phoenix II.

The wing of a Blackburn Bluebird being held up for inspection. Boulton & Paul built all the Bluebird and Blackburn B.2 wings, using a spot-welding process they had pioneered.

The rear fuselage of the P.64 mailplane under construction at Mousehold, 1933. It had been ordered by Imperial Airways.

The engine nacelles of the P.64, 1933. The company went to extraordinary lengths to streamline the aircraft to meet the specification. The plane was required to carry 1,000 lbs of mail at 150 mph with a range of 1,000 miles, all at half engine power.

The streamlined shape of the P.64 is best shown by this forward view of the aircraft taxiing at Mousehold in 1933. The Pegasus engines are encased in nine-sided Townend rings.

The sole P.64, G-ABYK, in the air over Norfolk. It was initially found to suffer directional instability.

On the P.64's third flight the lack of rudder response caused it to swing on take-off. It was tipped on its nose when it ran over a fence surrounding a cricket pitch.

The cabin door shown open as the engines are run up.

To solve the directional problems, auxiliary rudders were fitted on each side of the tailplane, as shown here. Sadly, the P.64 later crashed while being tested at Martlesham Heath. By then Imperial Airways had lost interest in having a dedicated mailplane, preferring to continue to carry the mail on their passenger services.

A model of the P.66 project, tendered for Spec. G.4/31 for a general purpose aircraft to replace the Gordon and Wapiti. Very advanced in concept, the P.66 lost out to the Vickers 253, which was only built in prototype form.

The P.71A Feederliner in 1934. Imperial Airways did order an airliner development of the P.64, the P.71A Feederliner. This is the first of the two built, G-ACOX, having its engines run up. The lady on the right, walking across the road that ran over Mousehold Heath, seems to have very little on.

The second of the two feederliners in the air. Both had very short careers, G-ACOX (see previous photograph) going missing over the channel, and G-ACOY (this photograph) crashing at Brussels Airport on 25 October 1935.

The pneumatic gun turret designed to solve the problems Sidestrand nose gunners were having in training their Lewis guns against the 140 mph slipstream.

An unusual view of the nose of the aircraft before installation of the turret. Originally named the Sidestrand Mk. V, such were the modifications that the new aircraft was redesignated the P.75 Overstrand.

The prototype Overstrand in 1933. This was the first of four converted Sidestrands. Apart from the nose turret the aircraft was also fitted with 580 hp Bristol Pegasus engines, a canopy for the pilot and a large windscreen for the dorsal gunner. Other changes were also made. The Overstrand was the last aircraft built at Norwich, but is regarded as the first product of the new company, Boulton Paul Aircraft Ltd, formed when Boulton & Paul's Aircraft Department was sold off.

One of twenty-four new-build Overstrands. They were the world's first bomber with a fully enclosed, power-operated gun turret. The Overstrand replaced the Sidestrand in No. 101 Squadron.

The mock-up of the nose of an unidentified project at Mousehold. It could be a bomber or a survey aircraft. The designers seem to have thoughtfully included a nail on which one of the crew could hang his overcoat.

The mock-up of a twin-Lewis gun pneumatic tail turret. It was designed for the P.79 project; a twin-engined monoplane bomber to Spec. B.3/34, which eventually produced the Wellington and Hampden.

The mock-up of a rather more remarkable tail turret, with twin guns in pods on articulated winglets. It was designed for the P.90 four-engined heavy bomber against Spec. B.12/36. This one produced the Short Stirling.

The shape of things to come. The wing of the prototype Defiant under construction at Norwich in 1936. The aircraft was completed at the company's new factory at Wolverhampton.

Mock up of the Horsa nose in 1941. In the Second World War history repeated itself. Boulton & Paul Ltd were brought back into aircraft construction because of their woodworking skills. They built parts of the Airspeed Oxford, and the nose of the Horsa glider.

Section Two

WOLVERHAMPTON

Hawker Demons awaiting delivery outside Boulton Paul Aircraft's new factory on Pendeford Mill Lane, Wolverhampton, in 1937. The company was attracted to a green field site, backing on to the new municipal airport. The Demon was the first aircraft built there, 106 being completed in all. Around six hundred workers made the move from Norwich, and there was a large pool of skilled workers in the area.

The directors and visiting dignitaries outside the main entrance, 19 May 1937. This was the day the first extension to the new factory was started. Standing, left to right: J.L. Wood (Secretary), Air Cdr. A.G. Gill, A.B. Bantock, -?-, Councillor Kidson, -?-, -?-, -?-, J.D. North (joint MD). Seated, left to right: Herbert Strictland (joint MD), Sir Charles Mander (mayor), Lord Gorell (chairman), Viscount Sandon (director).

The wings for the Saro London flying boat. This is the first set ready for delivery to Cowes, built in the early days at Wolverhampton. It was to return shortly afterwards when the driver made the classic error of passing under a low bridge!

After the Demon, another two-seater fighter filled the production lines, the Blackburn Roc. Boulton Paul built all 136 Rocs, and did the detailed design work. This mainly involved converting the Blackburn Skua to take Boulton Paul's own Type A four-gun turret.

Front view of a production Roc, 1939. The black and white underwing paint was a recognition aid for allied anti-aircraft gunners. The aircraft was useless as a fighter, being far too slow.

Rear view of a production Roc showing the turret, without guns fitted, *c.* 1939. Such was Boulton Paul's design contribution to the aircraft it was given their own project number, P.93. The Roc order enabled the company to build up and train its workforce on the new all-metal aircraft.

A close-up of the Type A four-gun turret fitted to the prototype Defiant, K8310, in 1938. This shows a slight problem if the pilot slid his canopy back when the guns were pointing forward.

The second prototype Defiant, K8620, 1938. The turret has not had guns fitted, and there are several developments to K8610, including glazed areas between the pilot and gunner, and stub exhausts for the Merlin engine.

Windscreen of the first prototype Defiant, *c.* 1938. It had a central structural member, but pilots soon objected, despite the fact that they had no need for a gunsight, as there were no forward firing guns. A one-piece windscreen was used for production Defiants.

A production Defiant, N1673, on a test flight, *c.* 1940. Note the aerial masts beneath the aircraft; the rear one retracted when the wheels came down. The Defiant is being flown by the chief test pilot, Fl. Lt. Cecil Feather.

Hundreds of women worked in the factory during the war. These are drilling Defiant skin panels, two or three sheets at a time, through a boiler-plate jig.

Defiant undercarriage doors having chocks and clearance members fitted. The young chap on the left is having to stand on a box to reach the bench.

Boulton Paul tested the original Defiant turret, which was a French design, in the nose of an Overstrand. Here the Overstrand nose is occupied by a 20mm Hispano cannon on a pillar mount, also designed by the French Company SAMM (Société d'Applications des Machines Motrices).

Assistant test pilot Robin Lindsay Neale about to fly a Roc. He had been a director and test pilot for Dart Aircraft before joining Boulton Paul as assistant to chief test pilot Cecil Feather.

The Boulton Paul Home Guard on parade outside the factory with fixed bayonets. A number of supervisors, like Billy Holmes (see p. 42), would not join the company unit as men under them in the factory were NCOs or officers. They joined the Tettenhall Home Guard.

King George V and Queen Elizabeth visited Boulton Paul, 19 April 1940. The royal couple toured the factory, and are shown talking by the flight sheds.

The second Boulton Paul electro-hydraulic turret to enter production. It was the two-gun Type C and was designed for the nose of the Halifax; it was also used for the Hudson and early Halifax mid-upper positions.

This late-model Halifax has the Type A mid-upper turret, and the Type E four-gun tail turret, but the nose turret is dispensed with. An experimental Defiant is shown in the background, possibly fitted with radar.

The four-gun Type E tail turret was the third main Boulton Paul production turret of the war. It was fitted to Halifaxes and RAF Liberators. Here it is fitted to a self-contained turret ground trainer in October 1941.

A close up of the rear gun mounting of BZ199, December 1943. Boulton Paul acted as 'sister' firm to the Douglas Boston and made local modifications.

An all-black Defiant night fighter and the three company test pilots in 1941. Left to right: Cecil Feather, Robin Lindsay Neale, Colin Evans.

An aerial view of the camouflaged factory, 1940. Defiants are outside the flight sheds on the right. To the left is Pendeford Mill with its pool; both are no longer there.

The snow-covered taxiway from the airfield to the factory, 1940. The Bellman hangars, supplied by the Air Ministry as extra flight sheds, are in the top right-hand corner. At the bottom is a blast pen, one of six cut into the hillside, but none of the five Defiants in view are parked in it.

J.D. North with a Type A turret in December 1941. He bought the rights for the electro-hydraulic turret from the French Company SAMM which had designed it, thereby laying the foundation for Boulton Paul's future in hydraulics and power controls.

The football team from the top half (nearest the door) of the drawing office, 1940. 'Batch' Batchelor, chief draughtsman, wears his manager's hat, and an apprentice, Ben Cooper, is next to him.

The team from the bottom half of the drawing office, with 'Batch' also in attendance, standing next to Joe Tovell. On the left of the front row is Don Lowry, with Harold Hill next to him, and on the right Les Cooper.

The women tracers of the drawing office, 1941.

Lindsay Neale (left) about to test fly a Defiant, *c*. 1941. He may be asking if anyone wants a short flight in the turret. He had a habit of doing that, instead of carrying ballast, and then putting the aircraft and its innocent passenger through every manoeuvre in the book.

A Type C turret under construction. Designed for nose installation, the large arched support member gave it its pronounced domed appearance when used as a mid-upper turret in the Hudson.

Mock-up of a twin 40mm cannon turret, 1943. The company built a number of cannon turret prototypes, but were never given production orders for them.

BA twin 20mm cannon barbette installed on a Lancaster, *c.* 1943. Together with the matching BB ventral barbette, this was part of a remote-controlled defensive system under development at the end of the war.

The prototype TT.III target tug conversion of the Defiant fighter, completed January 1941. Most conversions were subsequently undertaken by Reid & Sigrist at Desford.

A Defiant target tug in service with a Fleet Air Arm fleet requirements unit. Over 150 Defiant target tugs were transferred to the Admiralty. This one has a tropical oil cooler, and may well be in North Africa.

In 1938 Boulton Paul received an order for three prototypes of their twin-engined P.92 fighter, with a four-cannon turret. This half-scale flying replica, the P.92/2, was built to test the aerodynamics in 1941. The P.92 was cancelled when 5 per cent complete.

Wheeled trolley for Barracuda bombers in 1943. Following the Defiant the company built 692 Barracuda torpedo/dive bombers. Later ones were built on this wheeled trolley system.

An official visit in 1943 by Sir Stafford Cripps (second left), with J.D. North (right) standing by the tail of a completed Barracuda.

Model of Boulton Paul's P.105 project, a torpedo/strike/reconnaissance aircraft, March 1944.

Boulton Paul's Type D turret in the tail of a Halifax at Cosford, February 1944. It had twin 0.5 in machine guns and AGLT (airborne gun laying for turrets), the radar scanner being at the base. The Type D turret was fitted to post-war Avro Lincolns.

Boulton Paul's sports, 24 June 1944. J.J. Richards, the international Birchfield Harrier, wins the one mile invitation race. J. Hingley, the Staffordshire one mile champion, comes second.

The mock-up of Boulton Paul's P.108 Balliol advanced trainer to Spec. T.7/45. It had a Rolls-Royce Dart turboprop engine. It is shown here in November 1945.

The first prototype Balliol, VL892, 1948. It is flying with a Bristol Mercury engine because the new turboprops were not ready.

The second prototype Balliol, VL917, nearing completion in 1947. This is fitted with the Armstrong-Siddeley Mamba turboprop, which was more advanced than the Dart. This aircraft became the first in the world to fly with a single turboprop.

The port engine of a Wellington bomber being replaced after overhaul in May 1946. After the war Boulton Paul secured a contract to convert 270 'Wimpies' to T.10 navigation trainers. The geodetic structure of the fuselage is visible on the left; the fabric was stripped off and completely replaced.

Another view of VL892 in the air in 1948, taken from the company aircraft, the Airspeed Oxford, G-AHTW. This shows the Balliol's original rear canopy which covered a third seat behind the side-by-side pilots.

All Balliols had folding wings enabling the fuel tanks to be removed as here. Though taken at the factory the picture shows two RAF riggers.

VL892 fitted with experimental drooping wing tips in July 1948. It has also been fitted with the new sloping rear canopy.

Still VL892, but now (August 1948) fitted with the Mamba engine. It was one of three Mamba-powered T.1 Balliols completed. Production aircraft were to be powered by war-surplus Rolls-Royce Merlins.

Close-up of the Merlin-powered Balliol prototype, August 1948. There is a Mamba-Balliol behind, and behind that can just be seen the nose of a Defiant fighter. The identity and fate of this Defiant remains a mystery.

Boulton Paul's stand at the SBAC (Society of British Aircraft Constructors) Farnborough display, September 1948. The Balliol mock-up shows the Merlin-engined T.2 version, but the models feature all three engines.

Balliol T.2 pre-production aircraft, VR596, *c.* 1949. It is fitted with the 1250 hp Merlin Mk 35 engine, a de-rated conversion of the wartime Mk.27 Hurricane engine, huge numbers of which were available in unused, as-new condition.

One of twenty-five aluminium commando canoes built just after the end of the war, from an order for two hundred. They were powered, had a range of thirty-five miles and a top speed of eight knots. It is perhaps surprising to see these at an aircraft company, but Boulton Paul was not new to boatbuilding: they had built motor boats before the First World War.

Nose of Lancaster, ME540, fitted with the probe of Boulton Paul's gust alleviation system. This took corrective action with the ailerons when gusts were detected by the probe. It is shown here in 1951.

This Vampire TG276 was at Boulton Paul in 1949 to have its intakes and tail modified to handle the increased power of the Nene engine. The Lancaster in the background is again ME540, showing an earlier probe fitted to its nose.

The engine bay of the Vampire TG276 after the Nene was removed in January 1950. The company Oxford G-AHTW is in the background.

The Vampire being prepared for flight from Pendeford's grass runways in February 1950. It was one of the few jets ever to fly from Wolverhampton Airport.

The Boulton Paul apprentices, 1953, with a production Balliol as a backdrop.

The first of twelve Balliols for the Royal Ceylon Air Force, photographed in September 1943. It was the only export order received for the type. A Balliol T.Mk 2A version with a Pratt & Whitney R1830 radial engine was also offered for export, but jet advanced trainers were the order of the day.

Balliol CA306 being packed for shipment to Ceylon in 1953. Two Sri Lankan Balliols, CA302, and CA310 still survive today.

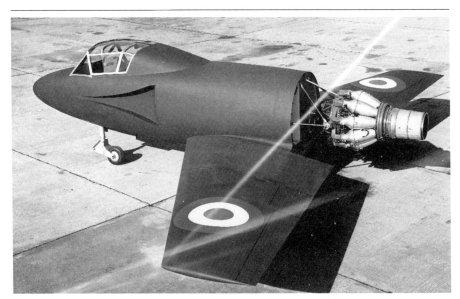

The elaborate mock-up of the P.119 applied jet trainer. It is shown in October 1950 with the rear fuselage removed to show access to the Derwent (or Nene) engine. The special NACA (National Council for Aeronautics) air intakes are noteworthy.

Artist's impression, dated October 1950, of three P.119s in RAF service. Sadly this was never to be; the RAF ordered the Vampire T.11 as its advanced trainer.

A Balliol flying through the Grand Canyon, December 1950. Two Balliols were sent to America to help the US Air Force assess the benefits of side-by-side seating, which the RAF was all in favour of at the time. More recently fashions have changed once more.

New chief test pilot A.E. 'Ben' Gunn, photographed in 1950 with a model of the shape of things to come on his desk. He replaced Robin Lindsay Neale who was killed in a Balliol crash at Coven, along with his assistant, Peter Tishaw.

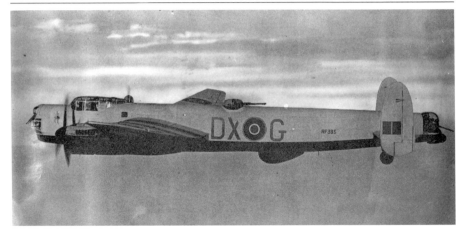

Avro Lincoln, RF385. The Lincoln was equipped with the BPA Type D tail turret, with radar, and the BPA Type F remote-controlled nose turret, but a Bristol turret in the mid-upper position.

The Meteor T.7, WL377, at Defford, June 1953, after BPA fitted a window ejection apparatus.

The Vickers Valiant photo flash crate being prepared outside the factory, August 1956. Photo flashes were used for taking night photographs.

The canopy of the P.111 experimental delta wing jet being fitted, March 1950.

Fred Crocombe, Chief Designer at Boulton Paul in the late fifties. He had come from Blackburn Aircraft where he had designed the Beverley. Before that he worked at General Aircraft and Monospar.

Fred Crocombe on a reef in the Timor Sea, 1937. The aircraft is the Monospar ST.10 airliner which he had designed. On the way back to England from Australia, navigation went awry and they were forced to land on Seringapatam Reef. They were rescued by a fishing boat before the sea covered the reef at high tide.

The second Merlin-powered Balliol prototype, VW898, over the Pyramids, 1950s. It was on a sales tour of the Middle East.

'Ben' Gunn about to embark on taxiing trials of the P.111, which is still unpainted, in May 1950. The aircraft was one of two ordered from Boulton Paul to investigate the delta wing.

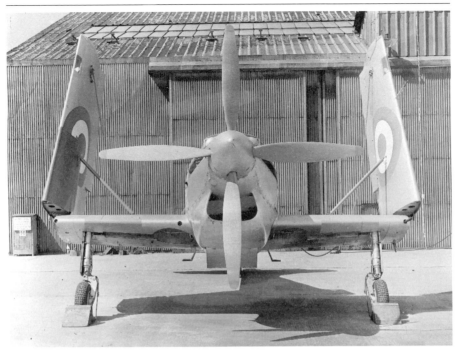

A pre-production Balliol in June 1950, outside the factory with the wings folded. Note the jury struts and the ropes dangling from the tips. These were used to support the weight and held by two hefty chaps on the opposite wing.

A Sea Balliol landing on a carrier, probably HMS *Illustrious*. Thirty Sea Balliol T.21s were built for the Royal Navy.

A Balliol T.2 in service in 1954 with No. 228 Squadron at North Luffenham. They provided mock targets for Bristol Brigands. The youth in the darker overalls is the officer in charge.

A group from the Empire Test Pilots School visited the factory on 8 August 1951. 'Ben' Gunn, himself a graduate of the school, is on the left of the front row, and his assistant Dickie Mancus on the right.

Boulton Paul's submission for Spec. ER.110T, the P.121, *c.* 1954. A twin-engined supersonic strike aircraft with variable sweep wing, it was well ahead of its time.

The P.111 delta taxiing on Pendeford's grass runways, May 1950. Flight trials took place at Boscombe Down.

The newly painted P.111, VT935, taxiing out at Boscombe Down in 1951. Fitted with Boulton Paul's earliest power control units it proved a very sensitive aircraft to fly, with a high performance for the power available.

A Supermarine Swift wing at the factory in the mid-1950s. Boulton Paul manufactured the Swift wings including the dog-tooth leading edge modifications.

The P.111 flying with intermediate wing tips. It was also fitted with pointed tips, and without tips, which gave it a slightly shorter span.

The company purchased an RAF Balliol, G-ANSF, as a civil demonstrator and flew it at the Farnborough Show. It languished in the flight shed for many years before being broken up by the apprentices.

During the fifties Boulton Paul developed a new system for the manufacture of a very thin, stiff wing, which it was thought would be needed for very high performance aircraft. Here such a wing is being drilled while held in a jig. The company's Balliol, G-ANSF, is behind.

The second of Boulton Paul's experimental delta-winged jets, the P.120, *c*. 1952. This has an all-moving tailplane set near the top of the fin. It is pictured here at Boscombe Down where 'Ben' Gunn was to make the first flight.

The P.120, VT951, taxiing out for a flight, *c*. 1952. The first take-off used an alarming amount of runway, as the tailplane had been set at the wrong angle. 'Ben' Gunn just scraped over the heads of some potato-pickers beyond the airfield.

The P.120 newly painted all black for the Farnborough Show of 1952, but it never made it. After only eleven hours of flying an elevon failed and Gunn was forced to become the first person to eject from a delta-winged aircraft.

Canberra B.2 At Defford, May 1954. From 1953 Boulton Paul became the prime contractor for all Canberra modifications, from the simple installation of new pieces of equipment to the preparation of new Marks. Defford was used for flight testing until its closure.

Tay-Viscount, VX217, 1958. Boulton Paul fitted electrical signalling to the controls on all three axes. It was the first aircraft in the world to fly by wire.

During the late fifties Boulton Paul did a huge amount of work on fan-lift for VTOL (Vertical Take Off and Landing) flight. This is their P.132 project for an experimental VTOL aircraft powered by four Armstrong-Siddeley Vipers.

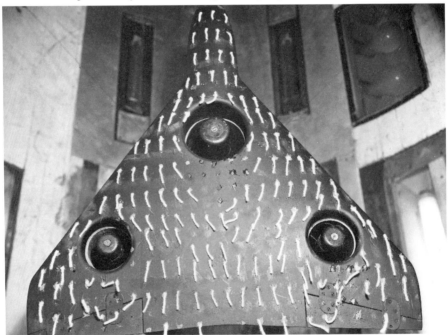

Tufted wind-tunnel model of the P.130 project, 1955. The problems of putting huge fans in the aircraft's structure were weight, excessively thick wings and aerodynamic disturbance.

MAIN CASING.

THROTTLE RING.

NOZZLE RING.

ROTOR.

REAR CASING.

A sectioned fan, *c.* 1955. The advantages of fan-lift were twofold: less ground erosion than directed thrust (like the Harrier), as fan-lift involved a larger mass of slower-moving air; and economy, as the propulsive power could be more closely tailored to cruise requirements rather than take-off needs.

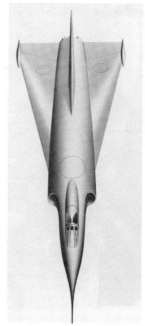

A model of the P.135B high speed VTOL research aircraft. It was part of the investigation of combat applications for the fan-lift principle.

One of the extra test pilots taken on for the extensive Canberra work was George Dunworth, shown here in the mid-fifties alongside a Canberra at Defford.

The Canberra B.1 prototype, VN828, 1955. It was the first of many Canberras modified by Boulton Paul with odd noses. In this case the long radome houses the GEC AI Mk.18 radar; the aircraft has also been given an intruder's cockpit.

The 'Stealth' Canberra, WX161, at Seighford, May 1959. A company flight test centre was set up at this airfield near Stafford. The aircraft has been partially covered with DX3 anti-radar material, as well as infra-red suppression exhausts.

A T.17 electronic countermeasures trainer in a hangar at Seighford, 1964. It is perhaps the oddest Canberra nose built by Boulton Paul.

A pre-production Lightning F.1, XG310 *c.* 1960. Boulton Paul also undertook Lightning modifications at Seighford, most notably the F.3 development programme.

A very famous Lightning at Seighford, June 1960. It is the P.1B prototype XA847, with the specially painted nose from when it was used for the Lightning naming ceremony. It has just been fitted by Boulton Paul with the mock-up F.6 ventral pack.

The cockpit of XG310 photographed *c*. 1961, before conversion to F.3 standard. All Lightning and Canberra work stopped in 1965 on the cancellation of TSR.2. BAC took back the modification work for its own divisions, and Boulton Paul's flight test centre at Seighford was then closed.

BPA also investigated VTOL for airliners. This early wind-tunnel model of the P.146 Project was photographed in June 1960. It is the last true aircraft ever designed by the company.

A model of one layout of the P.147, with a large fan to provide the lift. The company's last flying machine was for Project Prodigal, an army project for a vehicle with the ability to fly over obstructions like canyons.

The diversified nature of the company's work, 1958. Canberra intruder noses are being modified on the left, Sea Balliols on the right, Victor flash packs are in the centre, and in the foreground is a Handley Page Victor camera cradle.

A keen cricketer all his life, J.D. North is shown here (third from right) at the interdepartmental cricket finals presentation in 1967. Harry Whiteside, the team captain, is holding the shield.

Company football team, May 1968. The Company Secretary Geoffrey Haynes is on the right; Derek Hammond is the goalkeeper (back row, fourth from right).

The Beagle 206 being structurally tested at Boulton Paul, April 1963. The company built the wings for the 206/Basset.

The P.144 project, 1959. A six-seater airborne vehicle, this had two RB144 jet engines and four fans providing most of the lift. It was the ideal jam-busting commuter vehicle!

Lightning XG310 fully converted to F.3 standards, Seighford, 1962. Unlike the Canberras, English Electric provided all the test pilots for the Lightnings, and most test flying took place at Warton.

J.D. North (centre) in 1967 after fifty years with Boulton Paul. He was, by then, chairman, and was to die the following year. He was one of the great aviation pioneers. On the left is R. Beesley (Managing Director), and on the right Geoffrey Haynes (Company Secretary).

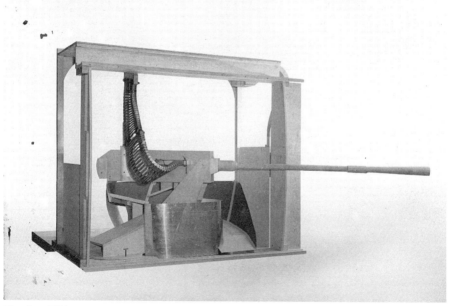

The last BPA gun 'turret', 1975. It is the mock-up of a helicopter door mounting for Westland.

Power control units being assembled in 1969. The largest on the first bench is a VC.10 aileron unit, and on the wheeled stand is a Concorde elevon unit.

The annual apprentices' awards and open evening, 1969. These were a chance for the apprentices to show their family what they did all day, and for the family to pretend they understood.

The apprentice school, 1969. Within the factory today are huge automatic machine tools costing several hundred thousand pounds, alongside presses which helped build the Defiant, and a rolling machine which helped build the R.101 Airship.

Dickie Mancus, ex-Test Pilot, in January 1974. He was awarded the MBE in the New Year's Honours list. His flying career had been curtailed, after significant technical input into the Tay-Viscount electronic signalling, by multiple sclerosis. He continued to work for the company but in the sales department.

Boulton Paul Sea Balliol, WL732, on display at the Aerospace Museum, Cosford, and the centre-piece in an exhibition of Boulton (&) Paul's history. Just over the rear fuselage can be seen a girder from the R.101 airship.

Two Balliol cockpit sections, having arrived back at the factory in April 1993 for restoration by the Boulton Paul Association.

Balliols, WN149 (front) and WN534, with restoration underway, *c.* 1993. The work is being done in a workshop provided by Dowty Aerospace Wolverhampton (as the company now trades). Both aircraft were built in 1954 (WN534 by Blackburn Aircraft) and served about eighteen months with the RAF College Cranwell before being sold for scrap in 1957.

Jack Holmes (left), who helped build Balliols forty years before, and Colin Penny, whose father and grandfather worked at Boulton Paul, removing WN149's fuselage fuel tank, 1993.

An aerial view of the camouflaged factory, 1940. Defiants are outside the flight sheds on the right. To the left is Pendeford Mill with its pool; both have now gone.

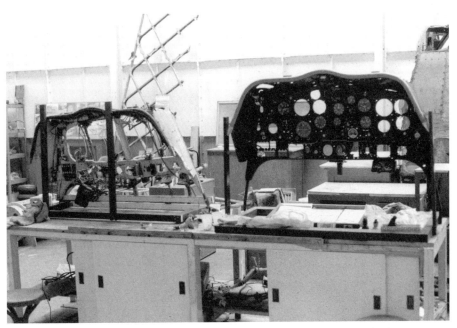

Before and after in one photograph. The unrestored and almost restored instrument panels of the two aircraft.

The Boulton Paul P.111A preserved in the Midland Air Museum, Coventry. One of only six Boulton (&) Paul-built aircraft left in the world, the others being the Camel and Defiant at Hendon, the Sea Balliol at Cosford, and two Balliols in Sri Lanka. The next few years could see that number increase with the addition of a Hawker Demon in Essex, a Barracuda at Yeovilton, and a Defiant at Wolverhampton, all restored wrecks, some from crash sites.

Acknowledgements

The vast majority of these photographs came from the archives of Dowty Boulton Paul Ltd, Wolverhampton, although one or two came from its former parent, Boulton & Paul Ltd, Norwich. There are over 20,000 negatives in Boulton Paul's archives, currently being catalogued by the Boulton Paul Association. These were chosen to tell the company's story because most of them had not been published before – at least not since the days when they were taken. A small number of photographs came from members of the Boulton Paul Association and others, most of whom are former employees of the company. For those I have to thank:

Alan Hague • Jack Holmes • Don Lowry • Geoff Monument • Miss L. North
Ray Sturtivant.

BRITAIN IN OLD PHOTOGRAPHS

To order any of these titles please telephone Littlehampton Book Services on 01903 721596

ALDERNEY

Alderney: A Second Selection, *B Bonnard*

BEDFORDSHIRE

Bedfordshire at Work, *N Lutt*

BERKSHIRE

Maidenhead, *M Hayles & D Hedges*
Around Maidenhead, *M Hayles & B Hedges*
Reading, *P Southerton*
Reading: A Second Selection, *P Southerton*
Sandhurst and Crowthorne, *K Dancy*
Around Slough, *J Hunter & K Hunter*
Around Thatcham, *P Allen*
Around Windsor, *B Hedges*

BUCKINGHAMSHIRE

Buckingham and District, *R Cook*
High Wycombe, *R Goodearl*
Around Stony Stratford, *A Lambert*

CHESHIRE

Cheshire Railways, *M Hitches*
Chester, *S Nichols*

CLWYD

Clwyd Railways, *M Hitches*

CLYDESDALE

Clydesdale, *Lesmahagow Parish Historical Association*

CORNWALL

Cornish Coast, *T Bowden*
Falmouth, *P Gilson*
Lower Fal, *P Gilson*
Around Padstow, *M McCarthy*
Around Penzance, *J Holmes*
Penzance and Newlyn, *J Holmes*
Around Truro, *A Lyne*
Upper Fal, *P Gilson*

CUMBERLAND

Cockermouth and District, *J Bernard Bradbury*
Keswick and the Central Lakes, *J Marsh*
Around Penrith, *F Boyd*
Around Whitehaven, *H Fancy*

DERBYSHIRE

Derby, *D Buxton*
Around Matlock, *D Barton*

DEVON

Colyton and Seaton, *T Gosling*
Dawlish and Teignmouth, *G Gosling*
Devon Aerodromes, *K Saunders*
Exeter, *P Thomas*
Exmouth and Budleigh Salterton, *T Gosling*
From Haldon to Mid-Dartmoor, *T Hall*
Honiton and the Otter Valley, *J Yallop*
Around Kingsbridge, *K Tanner*
Around Seaton and Sidmouth, *T Gosling*
Seaton, Axminster and Lyme Regis, *T Gosling*

DORSET

Around Blandford Forum, *B Cox*
Bournemouth, *M Colman*
Bridport and the Bride Valley, *J Burrell & S Humphries*
Dorchester, *T Gosling*
Around Gillingham, *P Crocker*

DURHAM

Darlington, *G Flynn*
Darlington: A Second Selection, *G Flynn*
Durham People, *M Richardson*
Houghton-le-Spring and Hetton-le-Hole, *K Richardson*
Houghton-le-Spring and Hetton-le-Hole:
    A Second Selection, *K Richardson*
Sunderland, *S Miller & B Bell*
Teesdale, *D Coggins*
Teesdale: A Second Selection, *P Raine*
Weardale, *J Crosby*
Weardale: A Second Selection, *J Crosby*

DYFED

Aberystwyth and North Ceredigion,
    Dyfed Cultural Services Dept
Haverfordwest, *Dyfed Cultural Services Dept*
Upper Tywi Valley, *Dyfed Cultural Services Dept*

ESSEX

Around Grays, *B Evans*

GLOUCESTERSHIRE

Along the Avon from Stratford to Tewkesbury, *J Jeremiah*
Cheltenham: A Second Selection, *R Whiting*
Cheltenham at War, *P Gill*
Cirencester, *J Welsford*
Around Cirencester, *E Cuss & P Griffiths*
Forest, The, *D Mullin*
Gloucester, *J Voyce*
Around Gloucester, *A Sutton*
Gloucester: From the Walwin Collection, *J Voyce*
North Cotswolds, *D Viner*
Severn Vale, *A Sutton*
Stonehouse to Painswick, *A Sutton*
Stroud and the Five Valleys, *S Gardiner & L Padin*
Stroud and the Five Valleys: A Second Selection,
    S Gardiner & L Padin
Stroud's Golden Valley, *S Gardiner & L Padin*
Stroudwater and Thames & Severn Canals,
    E Cuss & S Gardiner
Stroudwater and Thames & Severn Canals: A Second
    Selection, *E Cuss & S Gardiner*
Tewkesbury and the Vale of Gloucester, *C Hilton*
Thornbury to Berkeley, *J Hudson*
Uley, Dursley and Cam, *A Sutton*
Wotton-under-Edge to Chipping Sodbury, *A Sutton*

GWYNEDD

Anglesey, *M Hitches*
Gwynedd Railways, *M Hitches*
Around Llandudno, *M Hitches*
Vale of Conwy, *M Hitches*

HAMPSHIRE

Gosport, *J Sadden*
Portsmouth, *P Rogers & D Francis*

HEREFORDSHIRE

Herefordshire, *A Sandford*

HERTFORDSHIRE

Barnet, *I Norrie*
Hitchin, *A Fleck*
St Albans, *S Mullins*
Stevenage, *M Appleton*

ISLE OF MAN

The Tourist Trophy, *B Snelling*

ISLE OF WIGHT

Newport, *D Parr*
Around Ryde, *D Parr*

JERSEY

Jersey: A Third Selection, *R Lemprière*

KENT

Bexley, *M Scott*
Broadstairs and St Peter's, *J Whyman*
Bromley, Keston and Hayes, *M Scott*
Canterbury: A Second Selection, *D Butler*
Chatham and Gillingham, *P MacDougall*
Chatham Dockyard, *P MacDougall*
Deal, *J Broady*
Early Broadstairs and St Peter's, *B Wootton*
East Kent at War, *D Collyer*
Eltham, *J Kennett*
Folkestone: A Second Selection, *A Taylor & E Rooney*
Goudhurst to Tenterden, *A Guilmant*
Gravesend, *R Hiscock*
Around Gravesham, *R Hiscock & D Grierson*
Herne Bay, *J Hawkins*
Lympne Airport, *D Collyer*
Maidstone, *I Hales*
Margate, *R Clements*
RAF Hawkinge, *R Humphreys*
RAF Manston, *RAF Manston History Club*
RAF Manston: A Second Selection,
    RAF Manston History Club
Ramsgate and Thanet Life, *D Perkins*
Romney Marsh, *E Carpenter*
Sandwich, *C Wanostrocht*
Around Tonbridge, *C Bell*
Tunbridge Wells, *M Rowlands & I Beavis*
Tunbridge Wells: A Second Selection,
    M Rowlands & I Beavis
Around Whitstable, *C Court*
Wingham, Adisham and Littlebourne, *M Crane*

LANCASHIRE

Around Barrow-in-Furness, *J Garbutt & J Marsh*
Blackpool, *C Rothwell*
Bury, *J Hudson*
Chorley and District, *J Smith*
Fleetwood, *C Rothwell*
Heywood, *J Hudson*
Around Kirkham, *C Rothwell*
Lancashire North of the Sands, *J Garbutt & J Marsh*
Around Lancaster, *S Ashworth*
Lytham St Anne's, *C Rothwell*
North Fylde, *C Rothwell*
Radcliffe, *J Hudson*
Rossendale, *B Moore & N Dunnachie*

LEICESTERSHIRE

Around Ashby-de-la-Zouch, *K Hillier*
Charnwood Forest, *I Keil, W Humphrey & D Wix*
Leicester, *D Burton*
Leicester: A Second Selection, *D Burton*
Melton Mowbray, *T Hickman*
Around Melton Mowbray, *T Hickman*
River Soar, *D Wix, P Shacklock & I Keil*
Rutland, *T Clough*
Vale of Belvoir, *T Hickman*
Around the Welland Valley, *S Mastoris*

LINCOLNSHIRE

Grimsby, *J Tierney*
Around Grimsby, *J Tierney*
Grimsby Docks, *J Tierney*
Lincoln, *D Cuppleditch*